What's the Issue?

WHAT'S FREE SPEECH?

By Katie Kawa

KidHaven PUBLISHING

Published in 2019 by
KidHaven Publishing, an Imprint of Greenhaven Publishing, LLC
353 3rd Avenue
Suite 255
New York, NY 10010

Designer: Andrea Davison-Bartolotta
Editor: Katie Kawa

Photo credits: Cover (top) Traci Hahn/Shutterstock.com; cover (bottom) vystekimages/ Shutterstock.com; p. 4 Wavebreakmedia Ltd/Thinkstock; p. 5 Monkey Business Images/ Shutterstock.com; p. 7 Essl/Shutterstock.com; p. 9 (inset) a katz/Shutterstock.com; p. 9 (main) Jim Pruitt/Shutterstock.com; p. 11 Cory Seamer/Shutterstock.com; p. 13 mavo/Shutterstock.com; p. 14 Digital Vision./Photodisc/Thinkstock; p. 15 John Leyba/The Denver Post via Getty Images; p. 17 Rob Crandall/Shutterstock.com; p. 19 DGLimages/Shutterstock.com; p. 21 seb_ra/iStock/ Thinkstock.

Library of Congress Cataloging-in-Publication Data

Names: Kawa, Katie, author.
Title: What's free speech? / Katie Kawa.
Description: New York : KidHaven Publishing, [2019] | Series: What's the issue? | Includes index.
Identifiers: LCCN 2018002911 (print) | LCCN 2018002343 (ebook) | ISBN 9781534526020 (eBook) | ISBN 9781534525993 (library bound book) | ISBN 9781534526006 (pbk. book) | ISBN 9781534526013 (6 pack)
Subjects: LCSH: Freedom of speech–United States–Juvenile literature.
Classification: LCC KF4772 (print) | LCC KF4772 .K37 2019 (ebook) | DDC 342.7308/53–dc23
LC record available at https://lccn.loc.gov/2018002911

Printed in the United States of America

CPSIA compliance information: Batch #BS18KL: For further information contact Greenhaven Publishing LLC, New York, New York at 1-844-317-7404.

Please visit our website, www.greenhavenpublishing.com. For a free color catalog of all our high-quality books, call toll free 1-844-317-7404 or fax 1-844-317-7405.

CONTENTS

Speak Your Mind

The United States is a country filled with many different people who have different ideas and beliefs. These people all have the right to speak freely and share their thoughts and opinions with each other. This is because freedom of speech, which is also known as free speech, has been a part of life in the United States for hundreds of years.

Although many Americans strongly believe in freedom of speech, they don't always understand exactly what it means. Can you really say anything you want in the United States without getting in trouble? Read on to find out!

Facing the Facts 🔍

A 2015 study showed that 71 percent of Americans believe people should be able to say what they want without the government stopping them.

Free speech allows for the free sharing of ideas. This helps people learn.

5

A First Amendment Freedom

Free speech is part of the U.S. Constitution, which set up the government of the United States. However, it wasn't always included in this important piece of writing. It was added with the Bill of Rights in 1791. The Bill of Rights is the name for the first 10 amendments, or changes, to the Constitution.

The Bill of Rights was created to **protect** individual freedoms, or liberties. The First Amendment lists many of these freedoms, including freedom of speech. It states that the U.S. government can't make a law that takes away free speech.

Facing the Facts 🔍

The Bill of Rights was first **proposed** in 1789 with 12 amendments. Only 10 were approved by the number of state legislatures, or lawmaking bodies, needed to add them to the Constitution.

First Amendment Freedoms

freedom	What does it mean?
freedom of religion	Americans can choose what belief system to follow. They can also choose not to follow any at all.
freedom of speech	Americans can speak openly and honestly without the government stopping them.
freedom of the press	Reporters and other writers can share facts and opinions without the government stopping them.
freedom of assembly	Americans can peacefully form groups.
freedom to petition	Americans can ask the government for things they feel are needed and tell leaders when they think things need to change.

These are the freedoms granted to Americans under the First Amendment.

Different Countries, Different Rules

Some countries don't have free speech. The government in those countries can control what people say and how they say it. People can go to jail for saying things leaders don't like or for speaking out against the government.

Because of the First Amendment, that can't happen in the United States. Americans don't have to be afraid of being **punished** by the government for speaking the truth. Free speech means an American can't go to jail for saying something others disagree with. This keeps leaders from getting too powerful because people can freely speak out against them.

Facing the Facts

As of 2015, 95 percent of Americans and 80 percent of people from other countries said they believe people should be able to freely speak out against their government.

Many Americans exercise their right to free speech by speaking out about things they feel are wrong in their country. In some other parts of the world, people can go to jail for doing that.

WE WILL NOT BE SILENT SO THAT YOU CAN REMAIN COMFORTABLE

Free Speech in Schools

Do kids have a right to free speech, too? According to the U.S. Supreme Court, which is the highest court in the United States, they do. In 1969, the Supreme Court ruled that students in public schools have a right to speak freely, including sharing different points of view on issues.

However, students do have to follow some rules about how they **express** themselves. They can't get in the way of classes or other school activities. For example, students can't block the doors to the school when speaking out against school rules they don't like.

Facing the Facts

The American Civil Liberties Union (ACLU) is a group that helps adults and younger Americans understand the rights and freedoms they have as citizens and works to protect those rights.

It's never too early to start learning about free speech and exercising your First Amendment rights!

Not Always Easy

In many cases, it's easy to support a person's right to free speech. It gets harder when someone says something you don't agree with. In the United States, people are free to say things others might not like, and those people are then free to openly disagree.

Americans are also free to say things others might find **offensive** or unkind. Because of this, free speech is sometimes used by people as an excuse to say hurtful things. However, many people believe that just because someone can say something, that doesn't always mean they should.

Facing the Facts 🔍

Hurtful words about a group of people are sometimes called hate speech. In 2017, the Supreme Court ruled that this kind of speech is protected under the First Amendment.

Debates and arguments are part of life in countries that allow free speech. It's not always easy to respect another person's right to free speech, but it's always important.

13

The Right to Stay Silent

Americans have the right to speak their mind, and they also have the right to stay silent. Free speech also includes the freedom not to speak. In the United States, you can't be forced to say something you don't believe or feel is right.

Some people choose not to say the Pledge of Allegiance or sing the national **anthem** as a silent **protest** against the U.S. government. They have the right to do this, even though some people strongly disagree with their actions.

Facing the Facts

The national anthem of the United States is called "The Star-Spangled Banner."

14

During the 2016 National Football League (NFL) season, players began kneeling during the national anthem as a way to protest what they saw as unfair treatment of African Americans. This created a debate across the country about free speech.

What Can't You Say?

Some kinds of speech aren't protected by the First Amendment. For example, a person can be taken to court for saying hurtful and untrue things to harm someone, which is called slander. Also, in the United States, true threats are illegal. These are believable claims that someone is going to **seriously** hurt someone else.

People also can't speak in a way that will directly cause another person or group to do something illegal. U.S. courts make these decisions about what kinds of speech are protected.

Facing the Facts 🔍

Fighting words aren't protected by the First Amendment. These are words that can cause people to act out angrily. Fighting words don't add to the free sharing of different ideas. They're only said to hurt people.

The job of the Supreme Court is to decide how the First Amendment and other parts of the Constitution should be applied to the world we live in. This isn't easy because they were written a long time ago!

Facing the Consequences

Free speech means the government can't punish you for speaking your mind, except in very **rare** cases. However, free speech doesn't mean a person can say whatever they want without any **consequences**. If a person says something unkind or untrue, someone else has the right to tell them they think they're wrong.

Also, people have the right to be angry and even to stop being friends with someone if they say something offensive or hurtful. People can also be fired, or let go from a job, for saying things their boss doesn't like.

Facing the Facts

People often use the internet to speak their minds. However, some websites have rules for what people can and can't post, and people can be banned for breaking those rules.

Free speech doesn't mean you can say whatever you want without getting in trouble. The government might not be able to punish you, but there are often still consequences for saying unkind or untrue things.

Respecting This Right

Free speech must be protected, but it must also be exercised wisely. Having the right to say something doesn't always mean it needs to be said. In addition, other people's right to free speech should be respected—even if you don't like what they have to say. However, you do have the right to tell them you disagree or to share a different opinion on an issue.

Free speech allows people to share different points of view. When this happens in an open and respectful way, free speech helps make the United States a stronger and better country.

Facing the Facts

A 2017 study showed that 59 percent of Americans believe people should be able to share opinions freely—even if they're very offensive.

WHAT CAN YOU DO?

Learn more about what free speech does and doesn't mean.

Speak your mind about things that matter to you.

Listen to other ideas and points of view.

Tell an adult if you think someone is using threats or hate speech.

Think before you speak, and remember that just because you can say something, that doesn't always mean you should say it.

Respect other people's right to free speech—even if you don't agree with them.

Raise money for groups that protect free speech.

Free speech is an issue that's important to all Americans—not just adults. How can you exercise this right in the world around you?

GLOSSARY

anthem: A song about the greatness of a country.

consequence: Something that happens because of an action or choice.

debate: An argument or discussion about an issue, generally between two sides.

express: To make thoughts and feelings known.

offensive: Causing someone to feel hurt, angry, or upset.

propose: To suggest something for a person or group to consider.

protect: To keep safe.

protest: Something said or done to show disagreement or dislike.

punish: To correct someone for doing something wrong.

rare: Not seen or done often.

serious: Causing worry or harm.